Mythica

Also by Sarah Tiffen and published by Ginninderra Press
Learning Country

Sarah Tiffen
Mythica

Mythica
ISBN 978 1 74027 374 5
Copyright © Sarah Tiffen 2006
Cover photo: Robin Tiffen

First published 2006
Reprinted 2019

Ginninderra Press
PO 3461 Port Adelaide 5015
www.ginninderrapress.com.au

Contents

The Great Everywhere	7
What Lies Beneath	15
Song of the Ancestors	24
Song of the Western Line	29
My Father's Fruit	30
After the Funeral	35
The Invisible Web	44
Doubt	48
Midwinter's Night Dream	49
Ode to Spring	52
The Secret Precinct	54
The Question	58
The Dancer	61
The Turning Point	64
The Show	71
In Tribute to Theatres, Cathedrals and Architecture	78
Ode to the Quiet	80
Bonfire Night	83
Home to Die	84

Dedicated to my children
Tom, Lil and Wilbur
the bright, the brave, the beautiful
as ever

For Mum and Dad
thank you.

For Lachie, Greg and Elle
my dear siblings

For love

The Great Everywhere

I am built only of the blocks of soil and sky. I am but an imprint of
my country, tyre-track and hoof, furrow and row. I am tattooed in my
   soul with the juicy
brilliance of the light. I am nothing, slight, particled, riven with air,
holy. My body is the land and my kernel must shatter into dust,
and bring me into the everpresent, unutterable now. I am only this, and love.

That childhood! That everland of space and landscape!
Nothing more present than rock and soil, and sky, the bones of God –
the colossal bedrock now, my backdrop. That childhood before nature:
room for silences, eloquent as earth, as touch; myriad moments
stretching out in a sun-blinded aeon,
into whole seasons, that time and this, moments, thoughts, growing to
become the sum of all I was and knew.
My wide eye, my dark heart, always reflecting the mirrorshine
of earth and sky, the sweet rush, the oscillation of air
high up. I caught the whole, and perceived it
infused with the sacred gravity – deathly serious, beautiful, dense as
   dark matter.
I felt its weight.

I studied the sinews and gristle of the world,
the minutiae of blade and vein, particle, leaf and fibre, and
felt it, so far within me that it was but my own pulse,
illuminated in that bright pollen-cloud of light.
Through days of rambling, stalking, thinking,
building and cubbying, coiling and tumbling,
the scents of water, soil, beast, the textures of grasses, particles,
fabric and skins, taste of fruits and air,
the salt of tears. That childhood of looking down and in, and then
   uplifting
out in embrace of the glorious mezzanine sky…

Amidst all this, these flickerframes of memory,
always the quiet, the hushed, the held breath of it all
the undiminishing robustness, its pinpointedness
and endless frailty, the irreducible holiness of that unhuman place.

I, always watching, bore witness to the unfolding of the world,
in frames of dark and light. They winged my mind.
The sudden shutter forward to golden prisms of late sun,
through which I walk toward the halcyon western verge,
squinting into that light, which is a huge burst, a flare, a curtain
of dusty light, that blinding haze, that afternoon. The group of walkers,
stick figures, heralded on a
tall channel bank unkemptly weeded…or…
my chin upon the windowsill
and the whole grey universe of winter dusk drawn down
in folds of cloud, and I, almost sentient,
ordering the rain-washed sodden grids of land, the spectacle of
green, the fallen sky clutching and skimming the knee-deep
pastureland repeatedly.
I mapped it all.

I lived within myself, in poetica, mute, internal,
earnestly measuring the grand scale of landscape and space,
that time, and I, within it, febrile with the knowing.

*

That childhood! Tromping through the long days, legs on stilts,
hearts on swings, rent knees, hands grappling, the pack of big thoughts.
I fill with it – and see it still, a candlelighted, naked-bellied,
    watermeloned,
brownglass river and fiercely gathered heat kaleidoscope.
The long honey-crusted avenues of dream, the flying; it's all there...

*

One day as I walked the straight mile of red dirt to the hill, through
roadside grasses the colour of beer, I stopped suddenly, without
comment, and languished there, lagging from the party – we
were picnicking, or mushrooming, or was it flying kites?
(I remember the trees miles above my small head.)
Oblivious to calls, I stood, immovable as hills
and raising my eyes to the sky, and was gone.
The others turned from me – the slight, the nebulous child,
half-enveloped in the sweep and sway of grasses, the ragged
shudder of mulga clumps, who gazed forth
at the fresh-pressed heavens, the sky, that eye the sky.
They didn't know my danger then, nor recognise the look
that crossed my face, that pregnant rapture, as
I, in that childish instant, perceived suddenly the bright shift and fizz,
the cosmic web, the sheer miracle of atoms, moving in the gold
air in the middle distance, crawling in a gold static.
And I flew out to the Great Everywhere, perceiving all things at once
And soared in a current of great grief and greater joy, to
see and sense the wonder of that tremulous, particled world.
I could not name it, but felt it in my flesh and cells like a vast muscle of
penetrative heat, a fever, and an entering and washing.

It was that Great Everywhere All At Once revealed to me,
a gift from the land and sky, the light out there,
and I felt it only – it was beyond word.

Such could fell the heart, or raise it high, or both, and I, burdened with it,
burned with it in that moment. My eyes were coals…

I came back, to the others, and the
ordinary beauties of the day, which continued to its
close amblingly.
The residue of feeling pooled in me, a spent transparency,
but I feared not
for I was ingénue and trusting,
cradled as I was in the soft familiar,
the childhood of the long sweet light,
water-scented.

*

Later we drove out through the blue hills, struck out and scaled Mt Bunganbil, the sacred site.
From the top of that broken monolith, the thrust fist of the Colinroobie,
I felt it, god-conjurer, raised from the flat soil into the sky and looking down. The grid of
paddocks mile for mile in stucco blocks of yellow, brown, and green, and red and black and grey,
and snagged corners of blue, the remnant eucalypts, and sheep stuck round. It spread out
endlessly into the absolutely horizontal distance, and I looked down, at once close and far away,
and spread my arms out to that huge agriculture and ancient place.

And the pulse of that earth and the
jutted Dreamtime rock I had mounted, so rife with its concentrated,
    damp-wooded pepper, rocky rivulets,
strange waterfalls and bellbirds and caves' dark secrecy, drove
    through me. That childhood
jubilance, the jolt, the bright ecstatic urge, took hold, and sealed my
    longing, lit me up.
And I flew out to the Great Everywhere All At Once, and took the
    land into me, and
made my tribute to the everland of space and landscape that bore me
    forth,
And perceived the Great Gathering, which is also a Great Shedding,
    the Great Condensing
which is also a Great Dispersement, beneath the canyon sky.
I peeled down my layers and was exposed to the world, seeking that
    oneness.

And somehow, amidst the muted notes, the speechless gravity,
I grew hungry for the jolt, the burn, the bright
Ecstatic urge, to fracture me, and ooze my inward to the out, to merge
    me with
that great flat land that held me, hovering and slight, drawing,
    soaking my particles to
cojoin with the blooded loam, the steely covenant of rock, the giant
    watchful sky
releasing its unquenchable light, its throbbing open vein of light
    into the earth and all horizon.
I also, unquenchable in my silent thirst for that coalescence, that
    atomic oneness.
Perceive the thud-thud of it within me, in my belly and bone.
Almost too bright to bear.

*

For I was not shielded from the fear (it comes in stealth) and I
 perceived it equally.
Equal is the trembling, as for joy, as for dread.
(I feel it still – the spirit level always tremulous, seeking equilibrium,
which is *the* quest.)
Like a half-formed twin grown within, the darkness murmured
its hungry alien tongue.

At night in dreams I swept the flatlands, flying, soaring,
swooping down, skimming electric the rise and fall of plains,
propelled by the gravity of my desire,
joyous and in danger. The dead rose; I rose to meet them, and
walked among them soothingly, and flew above them,
and was beyond them and amongst them and mother to them.
Later I lay sleepless, locked in the black purse that was
my room, my bed, my heart, the night out there, staring sightless
into the black upon black.
And there, that same living static crawled my eyes,
not the gold, but instead, dark motes – dark, dark! – and
the stillness of crickets and wind rose in me
like a great thrumming, and I was rigid, reduced to
a kernel of fear within the enormity.
I know it, and I learnt it like a chant:

On the edge of the world,
the universe, the everything, and spinning into
that Great Everyhere All At Once, which is the abyssal night.
I stare it down; it seems I might dessicate and merge
into that night, that plenary dark. I will it.

*

Out I went into the spectre of the world
seeking the burn, the jolt, the answer to the Why?
This God, this death, this sacred gravity, this beautiful, this urge…
I had not the means to reconcile the everything within me,
and burned in the wilderness of that larger world. It swallowed me.
That innate joy, the core of faith, food to my blood like
marrow from those bones of God – the soil, the land, the majesty of sky –
could find no place to manifest itself.
It burned in me, and I burned out, and crashing, came to earth.

I fell from grace but then,
grace is only ever a precipice,
from which falling is due.
Daedalus told Icarus to take the middle path, but by his own
hand brought him down, and came only through this terribleness
to humility, to truth.

*

So blindly groping, drawn by the heart like a moth, a mole – that faint blip-blip
of instinct to the very source – the smell,
the texture and the particle and blood, the pulse and rhythm.
I chanced on it.
I came once upon my country and opened longingly, filled with the undiminishing poise
of all things there, and drank in the bright miasma of that same colossal sky.

I gulped it down. And wept, and fell upon my knees to give thanks before the
Great Everywhere All At Once that waited for me, ineffable, sacred and sweet,
and I recognised in it the pieces of myself I had left planted there.

For I am only built of the blocks of soil and sky. I am but an imprint of
my country, tyre-track and hoof, furrow and row. I am tattooed in my soul with the juicy
brilliance of the light. I am nothing, slight, particled, riven with air,
holy. My body is the land and my kernel must shatter into honeydust,
and bring me into the everpresent, unutterable now. There is only this, and love.

What Lies Beneath

The times made a benediction of homecoming:
and the history of the small town rose in a great wave of memory over me.
Corrugated iron roofs painted red of blood fold back like hatched hills.
Crows-eye view from the Hydro balcony across the patchwork of small lives in greens and browns, to the blue crouch of remnant rises, the fragment of faded sky.
Slowstepping in back streets and broken-heel lanes.
Their footsteps…

They are always there, raising their hands to the light,
bending their heads to the almanac brought from the Old Country,
Book of Days, shouldering shovels, shouldering loads –
farmer, soldier, shopkeeper and railwayman, seamstress, publican, swagman, orchardist, all in me.

Fast falls in blurring lines behind,
the westering arc of loquat light prising the main street wide with swelling wedges of gold –
everything suffused with the particles of radiant dust…

And there am I, fishing my hands through bright webbed visions,
seeking the vapour capture – flour-textured skin smelling of rosewater, tea-flavoured geranium afternoons, the wireless crackles over hot milk with Weetbix and sand sugar, buttoned-up Anglican chant, biscuits and pickles, and the washboard, and the sour smell of camphor, and apricots drying in sulphur smoke out beneath the cypress pine. It is always *The Sullivans*, tucked beneath the wing of her thin arm in the old lounge room, her quiet burp after tea, her soft lips and rollers, and him with his shandy, and *Auld Lang Syne* when you pulled the cork from

the singing jug, and the cool visitings under long, folded-back awnings; and
wool baskets, high beds and quilted bedspreads, lipstick on the rim of the teacups, many pourings.

Always the child, in that living past, squinting sideways into the tipping incalescent light. Always small,
and floored, floating, tiptoeing through the haze of heretic gold.
I pray.

These days make a sacrament of memory.
The levee of falling sun oils its way up redbrick shopfronts,
dissolving years, decades: but for the cars, and girls with bare bellies and piercings, it could be an older century.
There in the broken edges of the road, up the backlanes behind Madonna Place, behind where the Wade Club was, where Colleen brought her tiny child in the early days of grief, where the proud broken woman freed her broken husband into greater grief.
Grief, endurance and cunning, inscribed on brick and stone, in the staunch trunks of cedars, succulents' hardy masses scrunched in the corners of front steps and by small white mailboxes, brick-and-rail front fences,
hydrangeas like a beautiful clustering of cheeks and lips, membranous bloom.
These are the humble offerings and invocation of all humble things: the sermon
of small things made holy, an ordination of ordinariness.

Always the ghost of a school girl watching, sidelong and implacable, a gauzy figure shifting behind gauzy second-storey curtains, awash with the nectarous breeze, the deep mystery of secret longings there beyond the quiet breeze-rocked street.

'Nanna? Nan?' The sudden chafing thought almost leaves me and
  becomes a shout in the world, a small woman crossing the street
  far up, her handbag tucked, a certain disguised hobble of the leg.
'Grandma?' It could be, hunched forward in the little green car…or
  in Wandoo Street,
is she inside, just beyond the curtain in the front window, cooking,
  making lamingtons, maids-of-honour…listening quietly to pipes,
Stravinsky?
Its almost-ness is like an invisible rash on the inside of my skin,
  allergens working a severed limb, my heart.

*

Like a liturgy, the waft of lavender from the soft necks of older
  women sorting clothes in the backrooms of St Vincent de Paul. It
  is mixed with eau de old suit and mothballs, grinding pathos of
  'pre-loved' clothes new washed in cheap powders, dusty carpet.
Cheeks bear the runnels and gullies of tears-over-time. Shadows
  soak it up, and the clock, ticking steadily beneath the picture of
  the bleeding heart and longing upturned eyes, the simple cross,
  laminated prayer cards. The ghosts in the racks hang stoic-ly.
Further-out smell – the waft of the outlying orchards, sharp citric
  mingled with red dirt choke, arousing the heart folded open like
  a birth.
I can picture the great spouts of giant sprinklers, their authoritative
  flick-flick like slender reedy dancers, pirouetting above foliage,
  spreading water-feed to the thirsty orchards in a mimic of the
  prim kind Aeroplane lady who feeds her guinea fowl in the
  mourning river country, alone with the ghosty gums.

Women quietly bend to lawns, plucking weeds with walnut-
encrusted fingers, and men in polyester collared shirts and brown
shorts, their hair raked back and oiled like glistening leeches, roll
cigarettes and fold their knee-socked legs and listen to the staticky
dogs on the wireless…

Beyond, behind the wall, the empty yards, the stacks of tyres
groaning rubberly, industry's dispensation.

Sacrificial visions from the bygone rise from the flickering light. These
things:

twisted chicken wire; lonely tussocks of bleached grass; telegraph poles
weathered to splintery grey flakes; crooked wooden fenceposts, nailed
with sheets of corrugated iron; the resignation of cedar trees; the
borderland of broken gravel; redstone dirt; fallen cedar-berries' yellow
smear; staunch protrusion of staghorns; agapanthus; couch grass claw-
sly; Australia Post-red geraniums' sturdy bob; and grease smell and
rubber, and dust and tea brew,

and the older scent – an old room boarded up, the sweet musty
floorboards –

and cacti's struggling buried octopus all bleached from west sun;

then there's green glass vases and waterjugs, spidery vacuum-sealed
back veranda cane and cool green

and walking cane and a caul in a cupboard amongst crochet rugs.

Then come the pelicans flying high up in the slipstream, through
the high bars of the high church window,

elegiac white against soberly shining blue, turning and glinting like
tinsel on silk.

The whistle of the mill, the sturdy shunt of the freight train
lumbering its way east to a different century;

and beneath the bustle of the working man, the shadowland of the
Old People, their English ties, their finery and worn-

cream doilies and Victorian figurines, and Wedgwood, and crumbs
of afternoon teas, remains of the days, and a drip of green
water in mother-in-laws-tongue. See the sepia photographs of
handsome men on the sideboards, the unselfconscious joy, or
stern sobriety, in their long-gone eyes, women in bloom like
ineluctable Comtes de Champagne.
The Ancestors' apologies, their wishes, their longing for days.
They are there, see there! turned against the light, endlessly patient,
watching the world anew. See, handkerchiefs embossed with initials,
scented, flimsy, offered like prayer, waving, trying to catch my eye.

But I have to turn my eyes away,
the colossal pressure of loss like earth on my bones and breath,
heavy as sky, bearing down.

*

All this the tickertape of homecoming, the forgotten, thronging.
Remembered things suspended beneath the quiet surface of the
town, hovering, caught in the viscous light. The smell of hot
cement, and dust,
causes heart's revolt and the streets wind upon themselves; hearts too.
In the night, I wake to the half-dark of a waning moon, and I flail
up in an undrowning,
from the dreamed place…

What was the world I dreamed as I moved through it from behind,
as I straddled the scaffolding from now to then, and death a watery
undrowning?

It seemed I stepped through a lakey portal, floatingly, and a
glittery, shifting, golden glassy world absorbed me in deep magic
submersion. I walked through a house with yellow walls where I
had never been alive, but to which I was returning on this journey
– spare, with the high ceilings and deep bath and wide hallways
and a solemn, empty, consecrated air. The house was swathed, in
sweet peas' clamour, rose bushes grown heavy and wooded, and
butter-coloured grass. The garden twitched and flickered, a dense
chaos of summer life strung on threads and bobbing amidst the
predominant, glassy, anodised light – bright, shifting, dreadful
in its nostalgic ache – branches, plum leaves, bushes, passionfruit
and canna lillies all wavering and struggling and urging into gusty
winds, and dragonflies' bright fat notes, flying at random like a
million tiny bejewelled biplanes on sticks, just above the ground,
coppery, filigreed, creatures of the wet heat medievally scattering.
Oh the dragonflies,

And there, without prejudice, the Old People, the Ancestors were
welcoming me and showing me the way, guiding me through
golden light, just out of reach, gentle, strange, tangible. They
murmured gently, indistinctly in the ancestral tongue. And whilst
I basked in them, and floated through the murmuring world, I
tried in vain and could not catch their imprint on my skin, and
they were gone, gone, gone…

Oh what feeling rose in me from out of this vision, the terrible
flickerframe of joy, and sadness, longing, grace and love and fear.

Learning human, learning God, I fail my lesson, pay deep and dear,
my need and longing manifold increased.

Are they walking there, beneath the immovable present, its
   gelatinous veneer, shoeing horses and striding out along channel
   banks, tipping the combine high, bracing and hollering, cussing
   and calling dogs, sowing clover, pulling beer, pulling thread,
   brandishing guns, cooking and picking and weeping and praying
   and manning the cannery line?
What lies beneath this light, this wholly holy imagining: the
   roots and bones, the stone and lime, the particles of soil, the
   subterranean river, the God of dark, the storyline?
The bones of us, the shadow of a bird, what there? What of the juice
   and life, the canticle of toil and love that rings out just beyond
   the capture of the ear?
No answer but the singing roll of days.

*

It is harvest time. A hundred miles of honey-coloured stubble bob
   with the fat backs of grazing sheep –
wood-carved sheep buoys in a wooden stubble sea.
There are parcels of sky caught up on bricklebark branches by the
   library, and round the high school, skirting Black Park:
it is the jacarandas.
See their see-sawing song, their bright majesty – vivid as sea in
   the newly minted summer, vertiginous, mellifluous, their royal
   butterblue snagged in frondy shade. Arrested. Arresting. Blue,
   blue, the jacaranda blue – the drowning harmony, blue the eye
   that watched, the flying God colour, the condensation of all
   beauty to that single signal, rare angelic music-hue, ripe violet
   sighing Blue...
All abundant in the nascent summer bloom. Soothing. Beautiful.
   Somehow arousing the Spirit within the world.

Such a gift from those who planted indicate consideration of the
  continuum, reminders of humility, the weight of chance.
After the years of drought, the clenched earth, taut and fissured, has
  swelled and softened beneath the dance and drum of rain, more
  precious than oil, but equal to love.
What had seemed forever mounds of hard unforgiving dirt, the
  land's skeleton, has transfigured into tussocky sweeping pasture,
  riddled silky soft and yielding, another world, rife with wings and
  scuttle, caterpillar texture.
But what lies beneath? The same hard mound, the history of soil
  and sediment and buried objects and mineral and remnant of
  dead sea; the bones, the deep, foundation of earth and stone,
  shaped and inscribed by people, bones and blood, and shaping
  people endlessly
repeating the exchange of particled matter. Suffice this:
grain grows from the soil that holds the bones and blood of them,
  the Ancestors, the Far People, gone beyond the moment and
  enveloped in that mound of weighty loam, and so feeds us, and
  transfigures us and transmutes through us to the future, and so on
  down the endless line.
Some comfort there…but still, but still, I linger,
struggling, caressed on all sides by that which was, and is so nearly
  manifest in all the unchanged place, the homecoming.

It may seem as I stand beseeching on the broken carriageway of
  time that just for a fleeting moment,
the praying world may coalesce – just a moment, a trick of the light
  and the hour,
the minutiae of leaf and cell, particle and atom, a sudden shifting
  merge, a rush, a burr,

a swiftly fading vision, or a call not quite within the world…but
there, just there, just for a moment there before us –
the panorama of our dormant dreams, our memories, our history
like woven threads of gossamer, laid out. The Invisible Web.
That unclaspable, indivisible state of grace, the bevelled blown-glass
orb of the Past brought through will into the present.
I reach for it.
Like gold spillages of sun upon the surface of water, so vivid, so
solid, but then dispersed to nothing by simple movement,
ether between fingertips, a single remembered kiss: it slips away just
as it is reached,
the barest notion, slips, and falls away…
and in falling, echoes endlessly endlessly in the repeating silence…

The times made a melancholy of homecoming.
An offering.
A breath.
No turning back.

Song of the Ancestors

'Sell the Farm!' But we can't, not yet at least,
in honour of them.

They were the Old People.
Cracking the Darling on dray,
the bendings of earth jolt up pre-industrial spokes,
no shock absorbers in that shocking place and big gum axles –
now wheels adorn gardens, with gnomes and cactus.
Dwarfed by horses feet – giant clams, prance fringed topsoil breakers –
Great equine trains, deferential, blinkered,
Came the Ancestors.

Faraway perspective – Wilcannia,
'well, can ya?' – verandaed pub,
white chalky place outback Black Country,
pub refuges big as a railway station –
Big Thirsty, and Big Lonely, up in that
far pinnacle of the First State eaten-pie shape,
(alien for aliens from
Gaelic green and singing rains once;
or shipbowels mannacled) –
no place for the Angli-clans, immigrants
in long white dresses buttoned-in necks,
crinkle-eye scans the washed-out north for any
hopeful isobars, isolate, too late.
Some kind of detention, in the Centre.
Waterless ochre.

Unexpected odd mooring. Morning
Men came with suits, charts, talking water – divine! –
spoke of men making rivers spread out, pointing
government diviner-rods at winding transverse lines
on the big map – New South Wales, kiddo, its
a whole country in itself, a kingdom with every climate
everywhere…but here, here, here – pointing – it's water
wanting! So speak the forky-stick water magic:
McCaughey the Pied Irrigation Piper lures
with his water-chunnelling whistle tune.
'Take up! Take up!' Urging in sideways lips
to the postwar oasis. 'Make a killing, get yerself land.'

So, it was
water brought the ancestral lines to this brink:
simple anglo-peasants, roughy-red handskin, prolific,
devout, hungry for the few acres, with all the
broken soldiers and keen coves flocking.

Legend has it it was Mother (great grand) gave the nod.
God knows what lamplit talk in the back kitchen
bandied between she and the imbibing recalcitrant
Patriarch.
Children thronging and her belly stirring again,
had it up to here with pulling beers, she knew
shrewdly that this chance was it.
Him, stoned by the light, sought his unholy confirmation in big gulps,
rigged the horsetrain, bundled in canvas and water,
surrendering, clipped ears, cussing.

What followed was incalculable miles –
hypnotic, vast, hot, shoeless, hungry,
pressed by massive sky, down through the Unpeopled Places
and stations – almost unimaginable in these
cuckold days of flying things, truckstops, even telephones.
Wiradjuri watched carefully – the party
of immigrants immigrating beyond their own imagination:
one step, from mothersoil to gangplank, tongue-whipped,
months' long seafeet, unwobbled onto southernsoil,
the scrabbling round, roving, following gold,
lust, the promise of God or
drink, or water, the press of poverty.

(The future turned on a coin.)

They flipped a penny, at a fair distance
paused at the turnpike. Two roads diverged opposite from the one.
Eyed raggy children festooning the draytop,
cramming damper, wiping noses with sleeves – the little ones –
from out of the Old Country, faces as freckled as guineafowl,
   speckled as bush shadow.
Heads, right. Tails, left.
The left fall erased a whole right-turning
future bloodline crossing and mixing and fanning
out into the new century.
Not fated for the Mildura Murray flats
instead feted the Murrumbidgee lands, Murrumbidgee brown through veins:
Murrumbidgee, Murrumbidgee, the tumbling song of
PlentyWater/Plenty Full Belly.

Great grandmother, Matilda, waltzed so far and then Leeton
 enough.
Grandfather born, her thirteenth and last in the seventeenth year of
 the century,
in the calico tent in the quarry camp.
The war years, and the inland inured them to that great
 slaughtering.
An orchard kept them warless and wireless;
they carried it quietly, at the fenceline, a slight defence against defence.

*

On our selection, the family rose and rose and spread and coupled.
Witness a foodbowl rise from Sturt's bitter nothing to
this strange planet now –
dishwashers and airconditioning, packet cakes, satellite,
who'd'a thought? – and even the cannery closed by beancounters,
 when
its sprawling factory hours chanted the lifeforce labourforce anthem.

Now, having had two primary producers' wars, the delayed war
 begins, chiselling them, us, we, the family –
excoriating old farmers' prideskin, gouging the lines of helpless
 anger into foreheads –
This new war battling the Howard vendettas, the cohort of Vaile
 and Bush against the bush:
interest rates, taxes, cost of production, world prices, no tariffs
and the allocations, and trading and stealing, the Water Rustlers.
Only its the big end of town getting foothold in this smallend
 universe –
the Water Wars foretold in the prophesies, in the books.

Our stories, once great fat epics, doorstoppers, heart stoppers now
  pinched into penny dreafuls, plastic bites. Disposable.
They trade our words; it's dirty business.
The ringbarking spirit is indeed arrived, Les, and it's brought by the
  Right/Not-right,
They strangle stories in free trade, sneak speak and covert
  rubbishing.
It is a battle of language tries to write out the presence of the
  Ancestors…

And yet, and yet, they loom ghostly in the tribal places
church hall, paddock, park, cemetary,
beneath a tree, by a gutter and out out
beyond the water to the Far Flat Country.
The fight grows bitter for the past, for the farm and farming,
the old-fashioned agrarian socialism, and the Ancestors whispering
warning, on who we will become.

In 1910, the Tiffen family left the life of being publicans in White Cliffs in north-western NSW and travelled by horse and dray with their many children to the newly opening Murrumbidgee Irrigation Area. They lived in Crusher Camp, a tent town in the local quarry, before taking up land in Wamoon district.

Song of the Western Line

Gundibindyal, Pullabooka, Berendebba, Buddigower,
Gunniguldrie, Matakana, Erigolia, Quandialla,
Dirrung, Yarmawl, Gunbar, Quandary,
Goorawin and Murrami,
Kiacatoo and Gunebang.

Wargambegal, Mirrabooka, Morangarell, Wongatoa,
Beelbangara, Gilgunnia, Culpataroo, Thelangerin,
Yerrinbool, Booligal, Koonadan and Tharbogang,
Pucuwan, Bribbaree, Thudungara and Buralyang.

Weethalle, Tallimba, Ungarie, Yalgogrin,
Willbriggie, Widgelli, Euabalong, Carrathool,
Kamarah, Ardlethan, Whealbah, Toopuntal,
Tabita, Gubbata, Tullibigeal.

And Thulloo and Caragabal and all the unsung, and unwritten:
Songline of footprints, shadow of the faultline.
Language inscribed in the earth,
and the place-name story – history there in the
sidings and villages, homesteads, stations and
faraway properties, broken foundations, an old tank,
off its stand, rust and a tangle of wire, cities,
towns, forks in roads and sacred places.
Uttered without notice,
utter.
What do they mean, the rhythm, the poem,
of these ancient words? These whispers.
Of country…of history, what secrets, what struggle, what loss?

My Father's Fruit

Out of the blood earth, red dust,
stones like crumblings of rusted iron,
Coax the new tree.
Water.
Water.
Water.
Feed and water.
Mulch, manure, water.
(Without water there is nothing).
Submit to the honey light,
and prune as it grows.
The secret is in what you take away.
Remove those branches that will not bear,
or will leach from the sure bearers like parasites,
reducing yield.
Pragmatic and patient. Clip, clip.
Soil, water, light:
trees flourishing up into the sun,
steady, sturdy,
then a sudden eruption of colour and shape.

It is quiet and simple there –
sun, soil, slight breeze, one sonorous bird.

*

See the Garden like an Eden crafted from Desert.
Irrigation, and the mediterranean conditions
have made a Food Bowl from scrub.

He grew up quietly,
rambling with dark-eyed neighbours –
a Little Italy, shaped by the post-war.
Shared their pungent peasant feasts –
garlic, olive oil, pasta and grappa –
the European bent of mind.
The boy, drawn to the noise and warmth
followed the old Italians, who called
'Meesta Jammess' amidst the vineyards and orchards,
round the willowy bend of the road.

Small solitary son of the Settlers,
earnest, drank it all in.
He proved a quiet apprentice amidst miscarriages,
played in the dirt of the Orchard
at his father's, grandfather's feet,
Learning Fruit.

*

The language of fruit is earthy, spare, gold, with wind-chime rhythms.
Fruit trees are simple, following certain lines.
Prune and tend like this, and this, and then
see potential unfold.
There is a specificity, a relationship built on some certainties–
soil, water, light, quiet, seasonal lore.
Contained in the order is the split mystery, fruit's small miracles.
From one tiny seed sprouts a whole multitude,
many fruit full of seeds, many trees full of fruit, from the one seed!
and so on.
Like Family.

The Orchardist is prepared to play his part in that.
People are not so manifest.
Trees don't accidentally render you invisible in their grief.
Trees ask less, make their gifts without condition.

*

Retreating from the house, my father greets earth and sky,
it lifts from him, lightening and loosening.
In the orchard it's quiet and leafy.
Smells of life and sugar.
Under there the earth is clods and furrows where a boy
could rummage, dream and spread out secretly.
Girls might unfold and open like melons, or apricots, there.
At the right time, the fruit appears from flower and leaf like
an offering.

Look, Dad! I made it like you said,
but the old man is turned away, and can't acknowledge the small
    moment,
lost to the winds and sky, the business of the day.
My father carries this carefully, pruned off to stop the chafing, just this
    side of tears.
The years turn on, harden unsolved doubt, purify and cauterise the need.

Oranges

The house tree is small and squat
sunk in the dirt off the back verandah.
Unprepossessing. Source of life.
Liquid winter light showers it.
Navels, like globes of light,
Clean, orange, sweet, firm, cold with frost.

We bask in winter sun, and feast on these
jewels, citric, bursting.

Lemons

Shaped like an eye, hidden amid
towering plastic green.
Branches grow outward to the roofline.
Fish-like, perched in underwater light,
waxy, tart, big as emu eggs, fresh as stars.
Perfect yellow things.
Sherbet-ful, sugarful, lemony, rinsing.
Make the tongue sing, the mouth burst,
Sharply!

Pears

Europe could not produce
this ancient bell-shaped magnificence.
Royal teardrop, noble, forever paired
with nutmeg, gold and silver.
Pale and spotty like a freckled girl,
they nudge foliage casting a dappled medieval shadow,
hung like Christmas stars from cottage branches.
Stored in the dark in wooden packing cases under hessian–
they ripen secretly, plentifully.
Bite through thin pale gold to white flesh
Textured like some intimate liqueur.
Spring the wet sweet taste like a breath
after long submersion.
Juice dribbles,
translucent sugared tears.

Peaches

Only the old-fashioned peach,
darker than apricots, denser than nectarines,
with a fine fuzz, and the consistency of flesh.
The taste is a deeper infusion of dust and sugar and
brassy light. Firm, redolent, slow, and basking.
The peaches of the old days.
Catch them- they are like prayers.
Stout women, warm sundrenched bosom.
Hidden in the icebox they stay cool
and taste baroque, harpsichordant,
magic, grown in shadows, condensed nucleii
of land and sun.
Swinging in the hammock
beneath the wild magnolia, I eat them,
furtive, joyous, hungry, dreaming.

*

My father's fruit.
A certain method in a life lived
amidst the growing of food.
A kind of religion.
A kind of poetry.

After the Funeral

(Songs of the Ancestors II)

As we were coming in down Church Street
after the funeral
I saw her everywhere in the place
she had lived her whole life- on the
street corner, outside the butchers, on the footpaths,
and on the church steps, at the fishmongers, in the
lane toward her sister's house, and by the cenotaph, and there
in the park beneath the avenues of plane trees, huge,
straight-backed and gentle (giant aunts with arms
out-stretched and winnowing) and by the cocky cage–
(now filled with pigeons and goldfish,
and one sanguine turtle).
When I was at her knee, the cockatoos ate bread and
lettuce there, and rolled their little grey pebble tongues at us and
knowing eyes and wielded their claws as forks.
'Hello, Cocky.'
She was there, was it her,
just then…if I just reach out?
Small and thin in her dress of blue, her handbag
clutched in under her elbow, and her bent and swollen hands,
soft as paperbark, reaching for me as she smiled, the smell of
    rosewater,
and her brown hair set and caught in sunlight.
Longing's hallucinogen… If I am not careful I might pitch headlong
down the dark tunnel of loss, silent with panic, gripping air.

And the light was broken down into particles of grief
And drew out these painful splinters of memory, deeply embedded,
    like liniment.

A picture came to me then, of her geraniums, the sturdy Calvinist
   blooms,
That hardy cheering red of fire engines and old ladies' lipstick,
And the old-fashioned pink, like cheeks, and that translucent
   catholic white.
Bright, bobbing, and simple blooms – not beautiful,
commonplace, yet in their plain cheeriness, faces of centuries gone.
Climbing, they arrayed the grey fence palings at the bottom of her
   yard,
where she and the neighbour liked to chat.
(I never saw the neighbour's face, but recall a soft voice and
hands in gardening gloves passing things over – cuttings, fresh
   biscuits, wool
and photographs of grandchildren – the currency of womanly
   communion.)
There was one geranium bush brought from somewhere in the
   Victorian back-country,
from the hidden places of gold and dairying, to the world
south of here and nowhere
out past Gillenbah, south of the river country to the Hay Plains –
vast, spirit-filled and flat as board, immense and tussocky.
First struck and grown in the Old Days,
it still blooms.

Geraniums. Them geraniums...
To think the flowers and the fanning sour-smelling leaves from that
   one cutting
had breathed the same frugal air, and photosynthesised the same
   bright sepia light as
the Old People in the Early Times, the Ancestors of our songs and
   wonderings.

Those same plants, tended by the well-worn hands of the old
    gardeners–
those shy girls, mothers and milking maids –
wives of farmers, publicans, soldiers, renegades:
those unsmiling women in the old photographs,
staring.
All gone in a world of light.

*

We parked in the car park, where the Old Church once stood–
Place of christenings, weddings and sacraments, the sacred
Places binding and bidding down the years
(I recall somewhere within me, its magic vaulted light,
The fluted eaves, the air of stillness and grace in
Humble bricks and boards) – all torn down now, and replaced
By a new fortress of God against Modern Times,
the flag of St George in the ramparts.
And we went in slowly, the children, and Dad and I, into
St Peter's Hall, where I had been so many times with her:
The church bazaar, or crafty fete, or jumble sale, the flower show and
cake stall, brimming with treasures and plants, clothes and books,
Tended by the old women in cardigans and tweed,
Their kindly eyes, their great solidity, their comfort and Christian
    grace.

And as we stepped into the muted air of the Old Hall
onto floorboards worn smooth by a century of heels,
all the faces who were left of a whole Generation were there, and
their offspring, all the Descendants, a myriad of variations on a theme –
they looked up from tea and scones,

row upon trestle-tabled row turned toward me, and I drew back a moment
at the shock of the familiar
a sudden, visceral and unexpected recognition,
blood familial, yet a sea of strangers, like distortions in a dream,
and I felt as though I were drowning in a sudden rise of
unshed tears, and the unfamiliar familial bonds felt like a sticky webbing
that I moved against
silently.

It was a Clan gathered out of nowhere in her honour—
in the shared features and bone-structure, the eyes, the smiles and
broad hairline, a turn of the hip or chin, all versions of each other,
all the rural lineage mingled in,
there were hundreds there:
gentle women in muted tones, their hair set and pearls
about their bosoms, and husbands wrenched from paddocks
and into daysuits for the service, and the old landowners,
and merchants from Sydney, and importers, and the
well-to-do cousins from the cities, and the rural matriarchs,
the farm wives and the Italians and the Boardmembers and
church men,
and many the crooked heel of the lowly,
for she was friend to many,
and drew them all –
an unprecedented general impression of
old-fashioned formal grace, quiet
greetings and noddings, shy respectful questioning, their
offered cheeks, lace handkerchiefs, the honourable
murmur and mull,

as they trod the long road across this Earth,
to this place, this hall, this day, in Low Anglica,
humble, firm and stoic,
a crowd such as I had never seen; it was Family.

And then there was murmuring and rising with laughter,
and the wake grew convivial –
and the grandchildren and great-grandchildren played and
danced on the small wooden stage, and squealed
and squabbled in their little dress shoes, and rattled the
boards and wolfed the cakes –
and they ducked beneath elbows
and saucers, gleeful, wild, intuiting the import,
the adult emotion,
couples unfurled and mingled,
long-lost great-aunts, in-laws and friends from the old
days, gathering and breaking away, groups moving
in and through the hall, clusters, lines and circles, toward me and away,
and they drank more tea from pale green and pink and blue
   enamelled china,
and ate the cakes and slices, scones and sandwiches, prepared by the
   Anglican Ladies Auxilliary,
and unfolded their stories like old blankets,
handspun and quilted.

A bright, nostalgic scene
beneath a sweet September sky –
and I, with my belly heavy with my third child, and filled
with the unspeakable of life and death, sought
solace in the soothing murmur of my Tribe
gathering for the first and last time
on our sacred ground.

For this was The Great Mourning, and the Passing of an Era, a time and a way,
a manner of being, a turn of heart and mind, to God, to
humble things, a quiet stoic courage, acceptance of fate.
'She was a real lady, your grandmother,' said a good-looking man in his early forties,
a cousin of my father on his father's side.
He was a living embodiment of a photo of my grandfather forty years ago – a
stranger who I might have kissed and hidden in his arms.
I nodded.
'She was one of a kind,' says another.
'She was a good woman.'
Her sister turned her face and shook her head, pressing tears back.
And still, lost for words, they could only acknowledge this
simple enormity, the passage of the years,
the stealthy slip of change, the loss
with a shake of their grey heads, and recall an olden time,
simple, hard, and strangely sweet, like found wild honey –
(waxy, dirty, and with the risk of hidden bees, but all the sweeter
for it, and its own wild taste of dark sun, unlike any other) –
and a rural sensibility of thrift, privation, courage, godliness, privacy, community, prayer,
the full harvests, the floods, the horse-and-buggy days, the old-fashioned agrarian socialism.

We all felt it,
the gravity like a great flat stone pressing down.
And the bells rang out across the low town and fields.

*

To the cemetery, where the quiet is complete as hymns, and birds,
and the hum of sleeping ancestors soporific as midday cicadas.
The Mighty Silence rose up from the orchards and the vineyards
as we drove, as if the town, and more, the very land itself
had taken pause, and breeze and birds and industry stood back, and,
as in the Old Days, everyone who saw the procession stopped–
children in the school yards, and trucks full of grain, and walking mothers
with their prams, and old folk, all
out of deference, and bowed their heads,
bearing the gravity of laying this one woman in the ground.
The mourners gathered in carrying the scars and wounds of their lives –
their skin a lattice-work, hands and fingers like pieces of arthritic driftwood.
The Tribal ritual, the murmuring and tipping, the gathering and clasping,
the sense of gravity weighing down the sky.
Cars coated in the red dust made of particles of the past.

*

'I want to live,' she had said, at the grave's edge of my grandfather, fallen to dust.
Fifty years is an eternity to share a bed, and then alone.
'I want to live.'
And don't we all.
She would visit him, conversation murmured out across the bristling lawns,

New graves matched the dun-coloured paddocks beyond the fence.
  Her tears
curled into the leaves of elm and oak, the sad curlicues of
  stringybark, the lone crow
on sunfilled mornings droned in communion. She sat on the earth
  that held him, and her
brothers and sisters, her mother, her father, her grandmother, all the
  others – the whole
history of the Tribe contained.
She could not undo the ravellings of flesh and love between them –
  like a lost limb
he made himself real to her.
She lay down upon the red dirt mound that was him, spreadeagled
  and awry,
and shed her oldwoman tears into the earth, desperate, rent by the
  magnitude
of her fear.
'Come back, come back my love,' she whispered, dared herself, and
  pressed her
skin upon the soil.

Long after, she straightened, and brushed the red from her pale blue
  dress,
and walked off weakly, resolute – the dress retained the stain
  through three washes,
and she, stained by the experience, took on a new gatheredness, a
  firm resolve,
and told her grandchildren – 'I want to live,' and prayed harder in
  the old ways,
and some new, to cauterise her fear, her sense of falling.
'I want to live.'

But in her last years she succumbed to the pale grief of senility,
the silent mouthing, the broken heart, the
relinquishing of all she had suffered for.
It is the curse of the age, the capitulation to loss of meaning.

And now the town halts to mourn the Great Passing, to say
   goodbye.
'I'm sorry, Nan.'

*

After the funeral,
comes the deep vibrating calm,
the infinite quiet, the resonating air.

then the years of reflection,
the drowning, and then prayer for forgivenance.

In my memory,
I see her everywhere in the place where she lived her whole life,
The song of her, the lilt of days, the ribbons of life
streaming back from here, to the lightened sepia worlds
of the past, and the Old People, their simple dreams,
and struggle.

To drink from her cup, wear her coat , tend the geraniums
she watered, and
in the bright light of autumn, to take
flowers to her grave, and sit in thought
divining messages from earth.
What might come
after the funeral.

The Invisible Web

Cosmologists dare to speculate that ours is not the only universe, and that that which created everything we know of space and time could be just one of an infinite numbers of beginnings, yielding a never-ending sequence of universes, and the something out there, holding swarms of galaxies, cosmoses glowing with infinite galaxies, something keeps their stars from flying apart: known as Dark Matter, it gathers to form a colossal cosmic scaffolding, holding galaxies in place with its gravity. The Invisible Web. – *National Geographic,* May 2005

Pinpoint that moment in the light,
late May, late afternoon, ephemeral moment
infused by xanthic sun, the nascent winter glitter
in filtering glomesh of leaves' cold mirrordance.
The confluence of all things in that one moment, as the day cools
swiftly, air rising from the dry bones of earth, and sheep
walking the curtains of dusty light in ploughed soil
rich and dark as blood. Behold the gravity of that dying light, the
glorious fleeting splendour of the world, dusk's
imminent sharp descent.

Here, rising from miles of
purple earth spread and darkening, comes the revelation:
this is the glory-moment: the benediction of light,
the whole earth, and all within it
held up repeatedly, in that bright pollencloud of light
Appraised and loved.
Dumb beasts bear witness.
Follow their eye:
Here is an ordinary absolute – absolutely ordinary:
within this moment the act of being,
here, the illumination of the infinite beginning.

For this forsaken falling day, the sheep, the light, the spreading land
   and spinking trees,

the sharpening air
makes not a shape of awful power,
is not to smite us, or to fear,
it demands neither submission, nor quaking, but something else
　entirely,
simple, almost incidental if it were not of some other profundity:
notice;
receipt.

*

'They have not chosen me,' he said,
'But I have chosen them!' – Brave – Broken hearted statement
Uttered in Bethlehem.*

Something is taking place – it is praise.
Dusk as thanksgiving,
the expression of a godly gratitude...
in this lengthened autumn eve,
I see it suddenly – and try to find words to name it:
something wistful, more full with melancholy,
celebratory, gentle, reiterative, praising, thanks *to* us not *from*
is taking place
in this momentary confluence
this pinpoint of time within the dying light.

*

I struggle with the thought that sits within me
like an orb of light, impenetrable but translucent:
the Invisible Web contains me, and all things.
It is *in* all things, and *is* all things.
As the vision of the universe in dusty clusters of
nebulae and matter, eons and planets, galaxies
and systems, spread across the unimaginable vastness like a kind of
metastatic cloud, is, in its very wispy spreadness, a mirror of
the sky on any cirrus-clouded day on Earth, which is itself
the reflection of an x-rayed lung, a fibre, or life
forming amidst some few cells beneath a microscope –
the pattern within the pattern, a variation of itself, of the great holy
   themes,
the reiteration of some shared basic netting, which holds us all
within the space, within the crucible of time.

Is this the song of repetition, reflection and connection –
arteries like river systems, the brain like a world,
the heart like a sun, veins in the wrist's nape like the inner shape of
   leaves,
that branching.
A mackerel sky the mirror of the beach at low tide
with its undulating rhythms of ridged sand, ridged sky,
And more:
the scaffolding of the building blocks of DNA mimic
the scaffold of the universe in form…
the Big Bang that made all this vast matter
out of one small condensation of everything,

as incredible a notion as that reflected urge – a human made from one huge burst of
passion acting on the invisible seed that explodes to
shape a body and soul…
mirrored miracles.
a miracle of metaphor,
entwining all things, tugged and bound.

*

Amidst and above all this, a thought:
the absolute mystery of the world, and life, the
life within the world,
the rarest, precious indivisibility –
like a perfect stone clasped within two small hands,
round and smooth and imbued with infinite, unceasing is-ness.
Is this God, then, the praiser of all?

And here as the day capitulates to dark, in the ensuing hush,
the night sky is laid out as a great scaffold winking with diamond rivets,
and the beasts lay down and sleep within it
trusting the dawn to follow, trusting the Earth to stay within its orbit,
the heart to beat, the sun to fold over the horizon anew.
Behold, the Invisible Web.

---

*My thanks to Emily Dickinson for her thoughts in Poem 85.

Doubt

It is only the washed-out faded light,
The mackerel sky,
only the turning of the day toward
the dusk, the hint of storm coming in from the north,
cloud building and air warming, thickening,
the rising of wind, gustily, heavy with feeling,
making that shivery aching rush in pines and kurrajongs
outside the window, high up,
the late-day sadness soaking me like heated honey.
I am laden.
Only the smell of the years past,
and the quickening of all my thoughts and tears,
driving through me,
like the faded light, the skin-yearning,
heart-prickling promise hanging there.
It's breaking into me,
this lonely day, this time of wanting,
waiting.
I wish only to rise up to face the fate within me,
but courage fails me
in the face of this aching lowing afternoon,
the low pressure front looming in,
the thunderstorm building,
all particles electric.

Midwinter's Night Dream

In the midwinter, portent in the low cloud,
in the middle distance.
Cold folds in, close and thick, swathes of
replete, magisterial cold, wrapping down the day
the sky, the soil,
Muffling the light and any sound, awash in
the fogged noise, the winter held-breath.
The distance a frowned brow fumy with overhung,
whiskered mist.
The rain, a deluge, slanting in patterns, left-falling,
right-driving, verticle particleboard, wind-whipped
gusty and misty trickling and drowning,
drenching, bucketing, soaking, drumming
shushing, blustering.
This ancient, hills' dripping dells and undiminished
heavy sacristy of rain.
The winter, winter rain, bitter cold
looming and birthing the loam, that russet,
blooded loam.

Everything in secret, the eyes of the town
lidded and drawn, the sky as low as spires,
the paddocks cottage-sized, spawning green,
still cattle and horses, battening to it, posed at the
roadside.
The wood-smell and fireplace-haunching, socked-feet
and wet jumpered winterness.
Winter of my deep-rooted awakening, of my stillness,
of days of yore, that long-ago language,
the genteel, hushed greyed winter of childhood.

(Eyes watched from the flat sill the cottonballed hills,
the yearning cold, the drip-drip and spattery
rush of rain – like settlers we waited it out, closed in our
winter cases, the quiet crackling house, the quiet empty
streets, the thinking time; we watch through windows,
silently suspended, lulled by the hushing white noise.)
For aeons I have been in exile, so
even more, into the layers of winter. Winter!
drawing me in, in, into the past and dreams.
I ghostly go…

*

I remember this: one afternoon, it was winter
and I in my skivvy and jeans, sewed on the floor
with Mother – the smell of cloth, those weighty
camphored bolts – the jewelly insidelight,
dark daytime glow and glower and the children
tumbling and their baby shape in courduroy, and baking, and
the lace of cold on panes, in air, on me…
and other afternoons, walking down-faced and lank-haired
through misty loaming hours, the heavy winter gloom,
and the paddock – a wide cool silent stadium, where
my thoughts released themselves into droplet-ridden,
silent sodden space, a broad sanctity, open and
untethered. The smell of wet succulent earth,
the sheep clustered like pieces of ornate wood,
and I in my red parker, walking the long row out,
in a velvet muffle of big thoughts and
brewing love – the still and quiet times of my childhood.

(My need to speak became tidal then, and often ebbed
miles out, my low tide, silent and watchful, interior.)

And another, out in the hills, and crawling carefully
beneath the wire and through dripping bracken to the Coachhouse,
a relic of Cobb and Co, tucked beneath dripping breathing
gums and rising mist – the weight and smell of the old world
and stories thick and musty in the rooms and walls,
the buried glass bottles and pieces of china, and iron gates and old
    stables.
The hills rolled out in unexpected green,
glistening darkly, the soil like wounds,
plum-coloured and moist, folding out from the
lip of green, the mystery of winter cloud.

I walk those wet winter afternoons of my mind.
Sometimes the silence was heavy as lead,
as the bruising brow of sky.

*

And here, lifetimes later, this winter – the midwinter dark,
time of my homecoming, time of awakening.
The fraught air is low, draws in heavily
the low curtain of cloud – rich and grave, deep as a cavern of earth,
present, mysterious and visceral.
My heart draws in, too
as I watch the roan cows breathe their steam,
oblivious, complacent, dripping.
Enveloped, calmed.

Ode to Spring

The chimes on the top veranda yield to the rhythm of zephyr-winds,
tremulous warbling water-sounds, light as fingertips;
globes of sound swelling, dropping slaking into my inner ear.
The rhythm of the garden and the day is caught in the deep tunging of
    chimes.
Garden, sky, and see, there –
birds high up in the stratosphere barely moving and breaking
against the torn cocoon of clouds.

The languidly moving chiming day; sweet, sweet:
winter gently capitulates to the soon September – a gracious
folding down before the rising warm, the jonquils and wattlebloom.
The fat green pastureland nestles down in a wash of polaroid.
Gorgeous copper day, replete with the sound of small farms –
the drum of the small tractor-motor on the verge of the channel; the
    blur
of motorbike in distance; galahs' squabble, dog staccato, cows' low.
A European smallness of sounds, close andante, the steady quiet pace.

The sun is gold and warm: crystalline, divine, all the world
    hyacinthine.
Light, light, light, cascading from azure hills, lost in a Tuscan haze
of light-ridden blue. Sweet heavenly, uncapturably beautiful. In it
we are mute with quiet pleasure.
Simple day!
The air in the poplars rises, filled with the scents of earth and water
    – a bowel-smell,
rich and sturdy – the honey of seeds and life and pollen and reeds
    and ants and dung
and eucalypt and insects' pung and joy, joy, joy!
At this huge simple beauty, this unspeakable rhythmic chiming lull,
    the depth of urge.

I watch quietly
from the latticed balcony –
taking in the yard, the paddocks, the blue horizon on and out
to the sheer cliff of the burning violet sky.
I can't help but hum with that quiet pleasure,
a Godful humble joy.
Oh soporific, tangential, falling, brimming, sleepy, gentle
effortlessly beautiful day!
It dwarfs us and we are clustered beneath it, in that quiet, that
gentle, that unassuming warm.

The sun draws out my feeling like a liniment.
Bees drone soothingly.
The world is a honeypod of light, chiming a light, replete love.
Such easy homecoming.
Suspended here,
Wondering at what could have been
and what is yet to come.
But not minding, on such,
this soft day.

The Secret Precinct

The day after the choir night, I drove in a
trembling haze through the outskirts of town,
took the backroads to a new homecoming. I
passed the stately palms, lowslung verandas,
hidden porches rife with staghorns, ferns,
geraniums, village bends and crossroads –
untended, ramshackle, potholed.
Cars veer off as other cars approach.
The russet gravel verge sprawls, rampant
with bright weeds, asparagus and accidental plums and figs,
the old pines and kurrajongs.
I took in the secret precinct, that Fivebough,
its genteel lowlands, and all I knew.

I followed there, like a songline, that same small backroad, winding,
    unerring –
its rambling a prelude –
past the same silos, haysheds and cottage vineyards, the same water
    tanks and pipes,
same willowed nestling farms set back from the road and down.
So familiar!
Yet taking me now through strange country –
untraversed, heartwarm, vertiginous.
I barely recognised the landscape as I passed through –
my new eyes saw all the old anew. My skin, lately
tattooed with the heart-markings of that place, rippled
tinglingly as if veins of silver rilled and skittled
silverly from me, out to the bosomy clusters of rimpled hills,
beyond the canal.

*

The car clattering on the broken road, rattled, skimming the
ambling fenceline, that barely delineated the road edge
from the gentle trees. What secret lives in the lowroofed
houses there, in the patchwork of cradled pastureland tucked
in the crook of the hills?
The broken hearts, secrets and thrumming joys in the special
softened land,
saved from the vertigo of sky by those blue hills
lending the villagey nestledness, making the crooked
and cradled thing of it.

I brimmed with it.
The light like newly minted copper coins, then, a colour of the past,
windy, bright and high: my mind stripped and filled with a rinsing
clarity.
Such chords it struck in me.

It was the palette in that glistening midday, rang
the hammer to my harp. The light and colour stuck with jewels. I
drank it in:
the wetlands in the winter sun like a giant trembling mirror
throwing up the verging violet sky, some scudding cloud.
All over, scored with spirit-markings — sticks,
fenceposts, old branches, blackened grasses, tipped kabungi — a
scattered iron-filingness —
strokes, here, here, here, heiroglyphics against the moving glass,
and the shaggy gatherings of swamp grasses, leonine and honey-
coloured,
amassed for daily baptism.
The swamp waters lapped at the lower paddocks
like a great shimmering tongue.

Crop and pastureland romped to the very edge of the wetland wildly –
lavish, a rolled-out silken green – and trucking
back and back and up and back to the sky.

Oh that palette – the verdant vigour of green, so green, a reeking
distorting strobing green – verging blue –
then, further back, the purple soil, the pale paddocks, and the
bruised fallow, and the skimming pastureland, and still,
the wild synthetic green.
I hummed with it.
I sought the feeling in me there,
disarmed by
its sudden day-beauty, after all night visits, brightening and soothing.

*

One night, before, a tired face beautified by passing years, in the
    half-light of the porch
while rain fell like dust from the moonlit rumbling sky.
Shortly it bucketed down and the storm roaring in the poplars
made the big white noise. We were hushed.
We could only look out into it, chastened.
I pared back the membrane of illusion,
Bracing, and then another night –
the icy hushed night – which led to tears.

How many times have I stood like this in dreams
on the harbour of the porch
Before the huge black cup of sky, to see the stars
in their millions and billions, like diamonds
suspended in the gelatinous dark,

and us on the edge of it, witness-bearers to the holy
universe, and been moved beyond words —
by the matt night, the sheer air, the
yellow enamel of moon, the Dreaming Tree?

*

There in the Secret Precinct,
on the edge of everything, we
can only gaze in wonder:
the power of the bond,
the fragile poise,
the sudden comprehension.

The Question

In the deep midwinter
one came to me
and asked me, by the fire,
Why Poetry?
I said 'it *must* be, for sanity and
for pleasure of the word, to mediate the world'
And we smiled at this;
to have been asked;
to have been answered –
it was no small step.
A hand in mine feels warm
when all the world is steeped in cold.
I felt the
undulations of a pulse,
the ripples of that question,
out and out in the pool of me,
the pool of the future.

Moving

Five a.m.
Early summer.
Mother-of-pearl sky,
air with a faint whiff of cold,
of cut grass and water.
Birds' shimmering sound,
the long low chime of currawong,
choughs drawl, beneath twittering,
as dawn's pianissimo light
builds toward heraldic daybreak.
Magpies also, begin to warble,
once more, joyous to be, in a new day,
that ageless affirmation.
The babe in my belly stirs, weighty
as a stone. Two more sleep
in the end room, quiet angels, smelling of
skin and sleep, snoring, dreaming anew.
Two more nights in this house to slumber,
two more days till the trucks roll in.
We wait, as lambs,
our life in boxes.
The clutter and junk.
Was I dreaming of peace in a quiet suburb?
Was I caught in the crossfire of dialects preaching
me my way?
For my money, I'd buy time.
This move back into order,
seeking clarity.

To teach my children
the godliness of an early morning,
Early summer,
the Spirit revealed in the sky,
the right to joy, making magpies of us all.

The Dancer

That night we heard the old man speak language for the first time,
and saw the dance, and the dancer, made out of anguish and bones,
    made out of deepwater sinews
and grieving rippling snaking just below the surface of her skin,
    inside the marrow and the blood.
We were the interlopers drawn in to walk amongst remnant peoples,
    to turn our faces in sudden recognition,
and shame, bearing witness. It was deeper, beyond privilege. We
    groaned beneath the weight of it,
as beneath the weight of earth.

Later, the streets of transplanted Italy glowed eerie as we slipped
    from
the theatre's influencing grace; sideways glances caught
the lines and shadows, a neon moonscape of artifice, Jeffrey Smart-ian,
and the small ornatenesses, streetsigns' and shopsigns' ornate
    staccato – Il Corso,
Bellini, La Scala, Trattoria – and embellished balconies, and
    defiances of
green and red and white, and all the clacking black and jewellery and
    aromas
of garlic, cabernet and the lively gesticular peasantry of voices
    amongst smoke –
betrayals of the European.
We stalked on stilts of conspiracy above it all, laughing at bulging
    pubs and
the gatherings of half-cocked boys in alley ways.

*

In a stroke of luck, the car broke down at the edge of town; so there
    we sat in the shadow land,

talking talking on the edge of the Griffith Road, broad as a river, on
   the edge of everything, waiting in the dark,
and it was all we'd ever known. We saw
the bottle shop, Aladdin's Cave, and lonely cars full of Friday night
   desperates
driving the gauntlet to oblivion; the soviet menace of shadowed
   orchards and vineyards
beyond the Crossing. We dug away with sturdy shovels the hard dirt
   of the past
and future, liked the work. We waited for deliverance,
and did not resent its long delay.

See, you said, testing, provocative,
try this: a portrait of words,
a vision of the tumbling pantheon flickering before us.
Words, as before, come back to bind us, in halcyon days, and later
in lost days. The heart made the line, turned to a paragraph, into a
   poem
left to be found.
We ravelled words out there in the broken car, invoking language
to shape a land for us from this nebulousness.

*

Two days later the perfect evening drew me from the house and the
   stars were there as we'd watched them in winter,
and now early summer and a ripening feeling.
I thought then that I could drink it into me, and drink it down, the
   darkling sweet, the falling dusk,
water-laced air syrupy fine, all the evening world poised as an egret
   before it lifts away,

that new night air, soft and cool but undercut with warmth, as new,
    as dark, as sweet,
delectable as thigh, or lip touched in love, like petal.
I might avert my eyes from such sweetness as it falls, the silken sweet-
    holy, the
sublime saturation of light into water into scents into sky into stars
    into night,
pressing through the dark gossamer and through my skin, my
    memory blood.
Its frankness. Its archness.

From this words pool in my ear, residual.
We are left with these orbs of sound,
to weigh within our palms.
It will be the Language and the Land:
Language and land
Lingua e terreno
Dhaagun
Ngiyanggarra
Murrayarra
Dhuluyarra*

This might sustain the thought,
close the circle, be the seeds of our forgiveness.

---

* Dhaagun is Wiradjuri for 'land, or earth'
Ngiyanggarra: 'speak'
Murrayarra: 'speak out, speak loud'
Dhuluyarra: 'speak truth'
– *First Wiradjuri Dictionary,* John Rudder and Stan Grant

Black Seedz performed at the 2005 Indigenous School Students awards. My thanks and deep respect to Rayma Johnson.

The Turning Point

(Flooded by Light)
(For Mark)

Fifteen years gone in a moment,
And all things dammed up and forgotten,
Come flooding in.
I have held my breath for lifetimes awaiting this deluge.

Do you remember an evening in the church hall –
the vestibule displayed a visitor's book – did we sign it? –
dating back to 1933; an urn rife with hydrangeas'
membranous bloom, dark irises poised in flight?
The wooden floorboards, dusted the colour of sand from
a century of footsteps, echoed as we came in –
I, in my school uniform – it must have been winter, I can feel still the
texture of the stiff woollen jumper at my wrists, the tremulous pulse,
my legs in black ribbed stockings and my heart aflame – and you,
you prising me open, a boy in grey school pants, flamboyant, smiling.
It was a marvellous secret, that space all ours alone.
I see your hands upon piano keys – the old upright, stained with age
the colour of old teeth – your hands, strong, brown, coaxing music,
   smiling face,
the musculature of leg in grey serge. We talk and lark and talk and laugh,
skimming one another like stones on the pool of our conspiracy.
The light at the high windows turns darkling blue,
impressed with the diamonds of lamps and stars. Close by, the bestial
   crouch of
peppercorns, shadow of pines and kurrajongs, sagely, the limpid oily
   glow from
the old streetlamps, all bright and gold and brittle with frost.
I remember the cold – I pulled my scarf tighter up to my nose – but
   my cheeks

were aglow, warmed from within. You, teasing me. I climbed the stage.

The old curtains were a threadbare velvet, dusty with romance,
   history, magic, theatrical there
at the site of church meetings, Sunday school, Christmas concerts
   and CWA fundraisers, and
secret rendezvous. Backstage a Pandora's box of props and costumes,
   trestle tables stacked,
folded banners, pictures of the young Queen, and hymn books,
   chalkboards, odd shoes and tinsel,
smell of grease paint and hairspray and dust.
I took my place there, my lace-up black shoes hooked on the lip of
   the stage,
before the great space, before you,
Who, gently goading, started up a tune on the piano – so effortless,
   a craftsman:
carvers to wood, mason to stone, so you to that instrument,
   working it, made for it;
though it honkytonked for want of tuning, we didn't care.
You played, I sang: we were both surprised by my voice, it was
   strong and true –
you shone with it, and I, untethered and alive with discovery,
   coincidence, pleasure.
(That old hall had godly acoustics.)
I recall that feeling that hung within me then, a robust, shimmering
   rightness, that I have longed
for in dark days, lost in the wilderness of the world – the
   completeness then, on that night, and

we, molto sympatico, ebullient, laughing. What did we talk about? I don't know, but it meant the
world, everything, and contained all truth.

After, you dropping me off, we sat in your car outside my nanna's house for hours, knee to knee
on the bench seat red-upholstered, plotting, scheming, full of the wild future, full of the sweet now.
I try to capture it, the sense of it almost beyond words:
it was…the safety of belonging, the nuanced rhythm of our creative coalescence, the
muscle and sinew of our joy at the possibilities, the sweetness of being, connection.
I found lost pieces of myself in you.

We never spoke it aloud, but it seemed given, and I was happy, awaiting sacrament.

*

Do you remember those nights at the Old Farm?
Peasant warmth, rich in scents and glints, the european sensibility,
the smell of cooking, garlic, wine – drew me in.
Your mother smoking cigarettes in the lounge room – we
gossiped – where the window watched over
purpling paddocks and soft sky, a shelf of blue hills
in the middle ground, the gentle sinew of channels.
The risen moon was a pot of clotted cream above
the winding lanes of Fivebough, small hamlet, village,
keeper of secrets, Taylors, Greens, Youngs, Burns, Piccolos.
Your home country.
Your father smiled with dark eyes and quiet, his quiet

European grace even in overalls, his hands roughened by
farming, learned in the Old Country. From him to you, the
blood of Italy, your virtuosity, that urge to music. He eyed you,
full of love, full of doubt.
It was all talking and eating and laughing, it was the
just-rightness of it.
You, beside me on the piano stool writing music,
on the cusp of your genius; I, following, opening up my soul, and
absolutely home, hovering unwatchful on the cusp of my demise. How could I
know how not to fall from grace, unaware as I was of grace itself?
We laughed till tears came, and music rose like a clarion call
from us, fearless.
Later we sat on the roof watching stars – I doubted nothing,
you were out of reach but the stars were ours. I placed my secret heartfelt
letter in your hands and kissed your cheek and in the still dark
the whole wetlands, and you, on the rise, enamelled by moonlight.
Do you remember?

Awake in the dark together we spoke in whispers. I try to capture it:
it was quiet, but rapturous, intense, then drowsy till we slept,
side by side. I was bound to you, and you, you were flying.

*

The momentum rose and thundered – the night in the Grand Old Lady Roxy,
packed to the rafters, people in their best gear, children, grandmothers,
great-grandmothers, farmers brushed up in corduroy and cardigans, sceptics and

philistines, the rare arty set and the clapping like rain on tin. How
    we played, and I with spotlights in my eyes
rode your wave. We bowed together. The stage like a church to me.
I couldn't say what feelings bubbled up in me – I was ingénue,
    graceless, deeply moved,
and all at sea. In the confusion of the aftermath, hundreds gathering
    in the foyer, all the hubbub,
I found myself outside the theatre, Mother gathering me into the
    car, and as I drove away I
saw you through the glass, standing by the curb in your black
    tuxedo – a million miles between us.
Perhaps you looked for me, perhaps you looked far beyond for the
    sign of your future.
I was bereft:
these moments that loom within me even now.

*

When did you go? I lose track, can only bring to mind our letters,
    which kept me alive
in the long months. Oh such letters, that came and went feverish
    and desperate, your longing
down the long miles, in your immaculate manuscript style.
(It is as though words, letters, the very As and Bs, struggle to form
    themselves out of the idiograph of
semibreve, crotchet, quaver that are your natural language.) How I
    loved them, waiting for the mail, breathless
in the pinkish golden light of my girlhood. The paper inside the
    envelopes always scented with
the honeyed perfume that arrested me, the gravity of desire.

What passion passed along the mail route, in those tremulous
 anguished months,
from the dockweed-and-brown-water-land, the giant sky and
giant silences, to the clanging, tram-ridden, European glory of
 Melbourne, where I
pictured you, a thousand times, studious, battling with your bicycle
 each day, to the
Conservatorium then back to your aunt's house in St Kilda – the
 young artist abroad,
abraded and homesick. You were beautiful, animal, muscular,
 struggling
with the city which devoured you.
All the world and depth of faith were in those letters.
It was before the fall.

*

I was a long time falling, turned away from all that was good and true,
a slow motion tumbling out of heart and mind into aeons.
Do I barely recall that morning in my parent's house, I, smoking
cigarettes, lost to myself and bleeding? You came in, angry,
unanticipated. You didn't know
my secret anguish, my longing then. You berated me, mad with
 passion
and fury; I could not meet your eye. In my own madness, indignant
 and
furious in reply, I rose up and faced you in battle. It was my soul
you fought for, and I took offence! 'What right have you?' I flung it
 down,
and you, did you, in shock, in hurt, or in disgust, did you turn, in
 silence,

and leave me, silent and wretched, standing in the smokey light?
I recall only the shadowy echoes of the vanquishing moment.
'What right have you…'

But every right.

(I swallow my if-onlys, a bitter pill.
Who knows why the heart would turn from the one true thing,
 from sheer belonging,
darkly, deeply,
to seek more darkness, darker, darker, till the eyes are blind and torn with tears,
What shifting prisms plot and tangle us in the vast dark matter of destiny.)

*

I return now spare and spent, seeking something that I lost, and deeply need.
I am poet, mother, a spirit stripped bare.
I see you before me, in this liquid now, dissolving the years between us,
in the full flight of your promise: composer, teacher,
launching new works, testament to your vision. You appear to me accomplished,
a depth and polish, a weariness about the eye, but not so changed.
I seek you out, and falling humbled into the light, want only forgiveness.
Hope bearing fruit.

The Show

In trepidation, hesitant, but drawn,
I make my way to catch a secret glimpse of what is being made
inside that theatre, the church of the heart,
that Roxy, tucked there in the heart of the town,
by the cenotaph, round the corner from the doctors, the solicitors,
in sight of the old courthouse and the park –
the Grand Lady. I move toward the warmth.

Sunday rain falls upon the dark afternoon. Steely.
The light is that glassiest darkling grey, slicks of silver, platinum, pewter, gunmetal,
the anodised aching lonely light, sombre as prayer.
Oh Sunday, those winter Sundays, always the swiftly falling light
into the dark afternoon, folding down to solemn evening.

All the shops in the town are shut, they too folded down,
a general shuttered folding down, the smalltown hush, the mystery.
Only the Fisho
throws its yellow oily glow across the wet footpath and onto
Wade Avenue's riverbed of tar.
See through the window the busy turning and
dipping, frying and folding behind the high counter – the same as thirty years ago.
They wrap the greasy food in white butcher's paper
under flouro-light, ritualistic, tipping, salting and wrapping,
the shuck of sticky tape. I pick up that sharp familiarity,
that Sunday arvo, hungover, sore-bodied
quiet walk-through-the-glistening-enamel-of-
rain, the darkening sad, the darkling light, the familiar thing,
deep as marrow, the bolt of memory, destabilising.
The oily smell of frying rises;
I smell it and feel it, making my way in this new time.

So quickly does time fall away, and
only moments since the struggle of my youth,
those long, long afternoons and days and years
just washed away with rain. All gone in a cloud of light.

Elsewhere, in the religious quiet of the town, the footy on radios, late in the game,
mawling in sheds and on back verandas, the day of rest,
the lonely static of late-in-the-day winter Sunday.
Echoes of things past rise from the wet street
like steam, opening my pores to the longing.

*

The front-of-house, on this late Sunday, is closed and implacable,
ghosts of movie crowds silent in glassy shadows.
Through the glass doors, I spy the vinyl chairs,
spindly in their fifties poise, in the shadowed supper room.
The plastic flowers, and the high counter, colours
of the old days, mustard, beige and the chrome and gold, and rich
dark blue of the carpet and façade.
Sepia photographs on the walls show the outdoor cinema,
as it was in the early days, the days of
innocence. The foyer is still and clean, like a
painting of a foyer; the marble entrance, the stairs leading up through
blue velvet to the upstairs mystery, the dark of the dress circle, of the kissing and
fumbling days, echoes of memory, deep and longing,
the glamour days and glory days, the mandala.
I linger, staring through the voile curtains, the locked doors.

Then, rounding the corner, the full import of that building rises up in me.
I bless the great old wall of red brick – beautiful,
giant, and unassuming, hundreds of russet bricks,
inset with the brown-shuttered windows high up, closed to the light, rising up to the roofline.
I pass the poster boards, predicting future
excitements, the great signage of the Motel Riverina, and
the kurrajong trees by the taxi rank.

This is sacred site, place of many dreamings.
I am anonymous now, in this metallic gloom,
but oh, in the silent afternoons in my girlhood,
How I sat within these walls and wrote and dreamed of the big things, poured from my heart
And sang and dreamed and basked in it, and shafts of sifting golden sun shot
through the high panes and lit my hands and filled me. Motes of dust filtering slowly,
and the light, clandestine bright, that secret gold, shone into me.
I seek it again and again in dark days.

Then as I stand before the side door, the small brown door
inconspicuous in the great wall of brick, the old thrill rises.
See! I know. That door slightly ajar, on a wet afternoon, has meaning,
something happening inside, that simple door ajar
signals a promise of the magic within.
Something being conjured. I slip inside and into the shadows.

*

In the gloaming light, I come upon the secret world
that waits there in ether, now
Conjured from air, in that space,
rich and shadowy, older, echoing with whispers older than
that grey light, ghosts of shows past, ghosts of dreams,
lit by the eyes of children: dancers, singers, boys in jeans and
headsets, the principles and stage hands and light guys
and techies and chorus girls and boys; the Italian prima donna,
 slight and lean, in her
black rehearsal tights and leotard, her arms as fine and muscular as
 cats'.

It is all arms and legs, and the sweet smell of
young hair and sweat and preening. The lights playing, practising,
 the dance of the spotlight,
the curtains hung in their old familiar way, the velvet blue,
and the smell of dry ice, bodies and dust and
makeup. I feel the jolt hypnotic. The cast all watchful, focussed,
whispering, tittering, the excited frisson, sweeping the
seats like the wind to a sea of grasses. The girls in leotards and swaying
 cloth,
bird-like and lithe, repeat their movements, their song and sway,
repeating moments again and again, on the bare stage,
In supplication to the spirit of that sacred place.

At the high point in the dress circle,
the adjudicator's seat at eisteddfod time, the director sits, pacing in
 his
mind, tiger-like, watching, pointing, critical,
exacting, drawing the show like liniment from
the raw cut of the cast.
I watch, silently, unseen, listening.

Tears prick my eyes – from somewhere outside me.
I am taken by surprise, but of course… it is the past!
It is the music! The music, and the knowing, where it
sprang from the restlessness,
and the fragility…and the boy,
still here and grown to this…
even in the intermittent bursts,
the scattered disarray and adrenaline of rehearsal,
is a joyous surge, a sad winging down,
ecstatic, poised.
I soak it in –

Girls like slender reeds and boys as green and raw
and supple as saplings give voice and rise to this;
their freshness and ingenuity, grave and sweet – this one's
deep chocolate, this one's fine pointed grace.
They are children; and beautiful.
On the roof, rain falls like the spilling of beads from bright canisters,
or the pour of dry rice from jar to pan, the hushing roar.
The high roofline, rusted tin eaves of that high place –
the highest point in the low-risen town but for
the squat girth of the water towers on the hill,
their patient magnitude.
That roof line with its multitude of gables,
slaked with the shaken-shells rain.
I feel the spirit of the place rise up, answering the steady rain,
and soar – that spirit
flies up from this flat land beyond the spires and plane trees,
to the answering sky.
It is like gods to make a new thing. Holy.
And so wholly human and rife with desire.

*

(Later I will picture you, mimicking the
brolga dance beside a fire in a dark paddock – one huge
uplift of air with massive wing and away.
And you like a great bird bracing your heart for flight.)

*

At the end of the performance, the clapping rose and rose
like rain on tin, that continuous hushing roar. 'More!' they cried,
and 'More!' 'Bravo!' 'Bravo!'
The lights rose and fell and rose again, and the cast aglow spread
their arms to the glory cheers. The feverish heightened
vibrations of the final night rising and rising in air to fill the
cavern of that place. The jubilance of all the hearts and
faces there, filled as they are with the bright glow of the show,
their own power and the coalition of their outpourings,
their creation. 'Bravo!'

So there in that place of dreaming, place of
yearning, are all things drawn together into
the whole, each heart beating and the flesh and
spirit coalescing brilliantly and sweetly in
the shiny, sparkly magic world. What is that dark matter,
that cosmic scaffolding that holds us all,
and thought and love in place, and adjudicates the
pull of gravities and galaxies within us and beyond?
Elusive as the perfect cadence, is the dark matter,
destiny and, turning on a star, the truth.

On that stage, are prophesies foretold, and
coming forth, bring us out of our
dark days.

*

Later, the theatre, solemn and gracious, falls silent,
as the last footstep out the side door, and the last cord cut and
ribbon tucked away and the last of the glitterdust
swept up. It seems unreal to hear the silence fall,
the stately shroud of silence –
oh how quickly and how slowly falls away the
bright ebullience and young joy.
The stage is empty, shadows gather.
It is the air of promise, the older thoughts,
wearied, trialled and bearing the weight of the new wisdom.
Spent, but luminescent.
And the mind turns inward, awaiting the next
Great Leap.

In Tribute to Theatres, Cathedrals and Architecture

Llewellyn Hall is a cathedral.
Devotees flock – drawn together in rows
to sit and marvel at
architectural heights, the
music released within.
The ceiling rises to its own
acoustic vertigo – a virtue of wooden beams,
the skydive down,
swooping.

On stage a young man –
percussionist –
focused solely on the task,
pays his tribute to the whole,
the rhythm in his limbs,
his belly and his heart.
He murmurs to himself
speaking in the tongues of
tympanis, xylophones, bells,
and beating on.

He and the crowd are humbled amidst
the hall's largesse, the bigness of
it all, the music and in that moment,
soaring within the mighty space,
our futures.
A cathedralic crucible
conjuring the moments of harmony.
I worship quietly
the artless magic of his form,
his earnest drumming –

the way he has grown already
into a kind of manhood
from a mere motion within
(that church, that hall, that spirit place)

I am floored by love and raised by it.
To the rafters.
Thank God in the name of things sublime and tangible,
for love and sons,
all he will become,
for music and architecture
and what we all could do
in the presence of beauty.

Ode to the Quiet

Quiet
the solace of the introvert,
the great giver of space
for thought, retriever of
equilibriums, where the busy
and talked-out can rest, reflect,
and gather wherewithal.
Perspective rights itself
amidst the quiet.
The intricately woven mats of
composure,
logic and patience, wrinkled
askew from the day's scrabble, smooth out
under quiet. The floor of deeper doubts
is covered by their tapestry of order.
The quiet is a state of grace,
uninterrupted by other people's
output – the endless babble of opinion
which is this hypermedia world.
Quiet is a gift of nature, and the past.
Quiet, not soundless but
accommodating the barest and humblest:
leaves' hush, winging bird,
water running over stone, high forest whispers,
the sea's light supplication, wave upon small wave.
White noise, as clear
and unobtrusive as
the quiet.
Constituting it.

Quiet cannot uphold itself before
television, the discordant barking of dogs,
anger, people in a hurry.
These dismiss, bully, ignore or miss the point of quiet. Fear
curdles it. The crying of children rents it, but
children playing gently,
focused and companionable,
is the harbour of quiet.
Peaceful.

In the past the human mind basked in the Great Quiet
and its companion, the clean and quiet dark.
How can we imagine today the state of grace,
the unintruded thought, the implacable quiet –
without motors, piped music, phones?
How can we envisage the quiet day,
of labour, and thought, some talk and more thought,
prayer and contemplation of the natural world,
a benediction of quiet?

Today our lives are crammed with
saboteurs of silence, frantic and desperate.
We have become afraid of
quiet – though it is our salvation.
We live in liberated times, but our
minds are slaves colonised by noise, and
know not the freedom of the quiet past.
Gadgetry is quiet's pollutant.
Before the age of electricity,
quiet was plentiful – like
fresh water, and darkness.

Quiet must be won –
through resistance, retreat, insistence,
we must fight,
for quiet.

In the bush – the quiet reigns.
It can be seer and terrible in a mighty silence.
I have feared it, sometimes.
But without it
we are not wholly ourselves, and without
its familiarity, we become afraid of it,
and therefore afraid of ourselves.

But ah! The quiet is golden –
as poised as a bird, a droplet of rain.
Quiet is sleeping children
and rain on a tin roof.
Disciples of quiet find truth
within its great moments.
A gift we can give ourselves and teach the children:
quiet,
stillness within.

Bonfire Night

(for Peter)

The boy I knew
grew to be a man.
His core is now a steel rod.
With manhood comes
weariness, a confidence,
a wariness, and gravity –
worn in his stance,
the deep vulnerability around the eye.
He bends to his tiny sons,
the quiet, gentle touch.
They are made in his image.
He is fully fledged.
His is the firm hand.
His only fear under God –
to fail himself.
This man, compelling as flame.

Home to Die

I thought, when the pull was strong,
so strong from the earth out here,
when the light and air and the scent of it all
compelled me, harder than fear,
I thought when the call of the wafting sky
and the bright gold curtains of dust,
when that call came sudden, as if from afar,
but insistent, repeating 'you must',
I thought, when the weight upon my heart
was the burden of years in stone,
and the urgency of the yearning
was as deep as the marrow and bone,
I could feel it tugging me, quietly,
the rhythmic hungry ache,
I couldnt resist it, and home
was a journey I had to make.

But I wondered as I turned the tide
and drove like a lost one west,
I wondered and thought about that pull,
the powerful, driving quest.
I thought, as I placed my feet on that earth
and turned my face to the sky
and drank in the honey of home country light,
'have I come home to die?'

For it felt as strong as God-call,
as deep as the river and soil,
a gut-deep soulful urgency,
bigger than suffering and toil.

So it scared me as I fell silent
in the arms of the wide home plains,
to feel so desperately joyous,
so returned, more than faith explains.
And I thought my body had brought me
from the long dark wilding road
to settle my children in safely
then to fold beneath the load.
I thought that my body drove me
and pushed me hard to home
I wondered if I would then lay me
beneath the blood-red loam.

I feared as I settled my heart in that place,
turned my tearful face to the sky
and drank in that glorious home-country light
I might have come home to die.

*

Then the days unfolded gently
and the ripples and waves smoothed down
and the air was so sweet medicinal
through the low-rise lanes of the town,
and the children uncreased and unfurled
and their hearts grew lighter and free
and the torment that lurked in my tired breast
subsided degree by degree,
and the days turned into weeks
and the weeks flew from autumn on
and the quiet rhythm of farmland living
entered our hearts and shone.

And I felt the urge of the pilgrim
who had stumbled into the light,
the wanderer resting weary,
with the hope that the stars stood right.
By stealth did the hope steal over,
as I warily opened awhile,
I remembered to then move slowly,
and to breathe and then to smile.
And I didn't fold and buckle,
and I tamed the rising fear,
and I looked up, and sought to embrace
that which is righteous and dear.

And my equilibrium righted,
and my heart stood calm and still
and I opened my eyes to the present
and my soul began to fill
with the sweet bright liquid peaceful
and a new strength and courage there
and I started to shake the fear.
The days swung out sunlit and rare.

And I ventured a thought as I stood there
turned my eyes to the giant sky
that maybe just maybe He'll spare me,
and I haven't come home to die.

And then from the shadow of never
and the heartbreak of the past
came a new idea, just a kernel,
but one that could last and last.

And the tears and the joy of the longago
poured from the storm of my heart,
and I wrestled with my imaginings
and wondered when joy may start.

And I hardly dare articulate
the thought that then came to me
as I spun like a zephyr spirit
in the dappled glory of trees,
and I shied from it – it was beautiful,
and I faced it and shied again,
and I whispered it voiceless to angels
and wrote it with trembling pen.

Dare I say, as I took in the earth and sky
the big blue cavern above,
that perhaps I have not come home to die,
but come home to live and love!

So now in the face of danger,
in the face of the sweet unborn,
I must hope and pray and stay humble
that love may not be gone.
And I hardly can bare to wonder
if the prophesy may come true,
that I may have come home, to live, and love,
and this knowledge may bring us through
what may become turbulent waters
a sea of trouble and doubt
and somewhere when the storm is quelled
that it's love that brought this about.

May I whisper soft and patient?
May I dare to wish for more?
In this sweet backwater country
might I hope for a gentle shore?

So I wait oh so patient and passive
and look to the sky in prayer
and feel the life rise through me
and love, enough to share.

www.ingramcontent.com/pod-product-compliance
Lightning Source LLC
Chambersburg PA
CBHW062142100526
44589CB00014B/1657